What people

"It is high time, after La Rochefoucauld and Chamfort, that we had maxims of this quality in modern speech."
Andrew Sinclair, author and film director

"You show that a one-bite canapé can still be a gourmet treat, albeit one that leaves you craving more."
Patrick Kidd, Times journalist

"These are real gems. Bravo to the best Aphorist of our time!"
Gyles Brandreth

"A superb collection. One snappy aphorism is worth a thousand flabby platitudes. Feel free to quote me!"
Stanley Johnson

"Witty and concise… really wonderful… I will be reading them time and time again."
Ronald Blythe, author of Akenfield

"These aphorisms show the influence of many schools: here a touch of Pascal, and there an echo of La Rochefoucauld, but most particularly the happy inspiration of Oscar Wilde."
Donald Mead, chairman, The Oscar Wilde Society

Robert Eddison's

Wisdom & Wordplay

With a Foreword by **Gyles Brandreth**

300 original one-liners
to enrich your day

"To those who claim to read me like a book,
I'll ask what page you've reached."

Published by
Filament Publishing Ltd
16 Croydon Road, Beddington
Surrey CR0 4PA

Telephone: +44(0)20 8688 2598
www.filamentpublishing.com

ISBN 978-1-912256-26-6

Printed by 4Edge

With illustrations by Andrew Morgan
Cover design: Jade Wheaton
Book design: Clare Clarke
Editorial: Charlotte Fleming

Contents

Acknowledgements

Yes, I'm the author, but I'm also part of a brilliant team, with each member reflecting one facet of a very large diamond, without which the whole could not, as here, be greater than its parts. Those twinkling facets are:

Mohamed Abdelhadi

Gyles Brandreth

Clare Clarke

John Colt

Dr Julia Cresswell

Chris Day

Kenny D'Cruz

Petar Duraliev

Charlotte Fleming

Hocine Hakem

Deirdre Jalie

Pippa Kelly

Dawid Kotur

Sebastian Kotur

Olaf Kotur

Marcin Krysiak

Helen Lewis

Andrew Lownie

Susan Mears

Andrew Morgan

Professor Adrian Poole

Jonathan Pugh

Saleem Richmond

Alex Talbot

Zara Thatcher

Lea Turner

Jade Wheaton

Wendy Yorke

I feel like a balloon, thanking its life-giving oxygen for enabling it to rise.

Robert Eddison.

Foreword
by Gyles Brandreth

Condensing a philosophical or witty concept into a single line calls for great skill and mastery of language. As editor of *The Oxford Book of Humorous Quotations*, President of the Oscar Wilde Society and a lifelong lover of aphorisms, I know this to be true.

Apart from this author, I know of no aphorist, living or dead, who has originated so many high-quality aphorisms on such an awesome variety of subjects. As a taster of his larger collection, Robert Eddison's *Wisdom & Wordplay* is a dazzling combination of incisive wit, profundity and verbal dexterity of the highest order.

I'm a devotee of the works of Oscar Wilde, have appeared as Lady Bracknell in *The Importance of Being Earnest* and have written a series of Victorian murder mysteries featuring Wilde as my detective. For me, Oscar Wilde has always been the master aphorist, having reigned supreme for 130 years. Rare, indeed, is the man (or woman) of letters who could consistently match such classic one-liners as:

'What is a cynic? A man who knows the price of everything and the value of nothing' or

'Philosophy teaches us to bear with equanimity the misfortunes of others'

But, although not all gods reign for eternity, it never once occurred to me that this particular one could ever be dethroned – until now. Could it just be that, in the author of this remarkable book, Wilde has finally met his match?

I am proud to introduce you to Robert Eddison. How should I describe him? While reading Modern Languages and Law at Cambridge, he won a European scholarship, which was followed by a university lectureship and a Foreign Office consultancy. But it's his lifelong fascination with the written and spoken word that has dictated Robert's two main hobbies – coining mint-fresh aphorisms and public speaking, which led to some freelance broadcasting for the BBC and a lecture tour of America.

And it was Robert's Puckish love of words and wordplay that finally drew him to a career in mainstream journalism, writing periodic colour features for the broadsheets and tabloids. As a lifelong member of Mensa, he also chairs some of its popular discussion dinners and was recently appointed to a directorship of the newly formed international charity for high ability (IAFHA), which seeks to identify and nurture gifted children.

Robert's love of words is, of course, widely shared by other journalists and public figures, who, like me, are constantly on the lookout for new material to add a dash of sparkle to their speeches and lectures. This treasure-house of highly individual quotes provides a rich source of ideas, be it for us, the best man at a wedding or the conference delegate.

This book also offers the ideal year-round gift for every lover of words. It's a book to live with and savour, like a good liqueur, line by glorious line. You'll need *three* copies, though – one as a gift, one for your travelling bag and one for the loo.

For me, Robert is *the* Aphorist – a wise, witty and deeply thoughtful observer of our times. He isn't Wilde. He's Eddison. And quite wonderful.

You have his book in your hands and you'll soon have his aphorisms in your head.

Enjoy them. They are the best.

Wordplay

Squares are never ahead
of the curve

The nicotine addict with money to burn
can only watch it go up in smoke

Wooden people lack polish

Some broken English is broken
beyond repair

Leading the simple life can be
very complicated

Throwaway remarks are
not always caught

The professional heckler is a weapon
of mass disruption

Rush your fences and you could be
in for the high jump

No ageing diva wants to be seen
in a good light

Loosened purse strings can lead to
tight budgets

The death of old habits
usually follows a long illness

There is no denying that those in
denial will deny being there

The single-minded are often two-faced

The absent-minded professor
is not so much absent
as present elsewhere

Soft touches are toast to those who
butter them up

Cheap thrills can come expensive

Naked ambition rarely parades
itself unclothed

The rich needn't trade on their looks
to sit pretty

The spendthrift is more spend
than thrift

No insomniac can sleep on it

With not a single possession to their name, fish get along swimmingly

It's hard to lick your wounds after being stabbed in the back

Circles are best squared when you don't go around in them

In a well-cleaned home, no job bites the dust

One sometimes has to lie
to be honest

Trust, like money,
must be carefully invested

If youth binges on adventure,
age fasts on risk

Every puppeteer pulls strings to get to the top

If repetition kills conversation,
it gives life to music

You never have to look far
to find your feet

In bear markets,
gold likes to show its mettle

Even the best-fitting dentures have
their teething problems

There's no point turning the screw
before you've nailed your victim

When their shares go through the floor,
investors hit the roof

Few bang the drum for those
who blow their own trumpet

———————◆———————

To gluttons, the dessert is always
worth the weight

———————◆———————

In hard times, banks serve their
customers with little interest

———————◆———————

Circular discussions end up at square one

Endangered species should
only be shot with a camera

◆

Peeing is relieving

◆

It's during their salad days that most
young matadors get tossed

◆

All broadcasters have the
face for radio

Denial protects the parts
that reason cannot reach

Beware the surgeon
who asks for your hand

The moon was never designed to put
stars into lovers' eyes

For gossips, getting wind of a scandal
is a breeze

Pregnant pauses
don't always deliver

It takes an archaeologist to build
from the ground down

Running jokes
can soon end up limping

Those in the hot seat should stay cool

Reflective

Most careers bubble happily along
without the kettle ever whistling

———————◆———————

The curious are their own best teachers

———————◆———————

You may watch a tree grow for ten years,
but you will never see it growing

———————◆———————

Only when happy in your own skin can
you put yourself in another's

A clear conscience makes the
best sleeping pill

We all want to be understood -
but not too well

Verbosity acts like a weed
to throttle meaning

Deep thoughts take time to surface

Not being yourself is part of
being yourself

The older our skin,
the more comfortable we feel in it

Modesty comes from seeing
ourselves in perspective

Poverty is both brake and spur
to ambition

There is no greater tyrant than convention

A breakdown can lead to
a breakthrough

Rules are quickest learnt
when broken

Those who spend their time telling us
how busy they are get little done

Most seats of power are
too well upholstered

We only allow facts to speak for
themselves when we like
what they say

If you can't have what you want, you'd better
want what you have

Fools pontificate with the
full authority of ignorance

Stopping children from making
mistakes is itself a mistake

Staying lucky is hard work

Youth holds little joy unless wasted

Beware the man who is in charge
of others, but not of himself

What we regret we cannot own

Offence given need not be taken

Only what leaves your heart
can reach another's

We are at the mercy of
what we don't confront

Ignorance is no more bliss
than a vacuum

Every religion is but a single colour on
the rainbow of speculation

Those with a way with words
usually get their way

We learn fastest doing what we love

You won't get on with others until you get
on with yourself

Food is best flavoured with the
salt of conversation

Look after the children and the
adults will look after themselves

Denial is the mind's preferred painkiller

It's hard to forget
what we really understand

You can't be under the weather
if you're over the moon

The more we have to live for,
the longer we live

Wisdom is what remains after we've
forgotten how we acquired it

Speaking your mind makes for
better conversation than
minding your speech

Fate is the label we stick on our failures;
for our successes, we take full credit

The quicker we get to the bottom
of things, the quicker we
rise to the top

Gossips like to hang out another's
dirty linen before it's washed

Embarrassment likes to cover itself
in laughter's duvet

It's only at funerals that we see our friends'
lives in the round

Justice is mainly lauded
by those it exonerates

Charisma switches on the
light inside you

Every original thought has its ancestors

We only regret the failures that
we didn't turn into blessings

Dark

Even in death, people can loom
larger than life

———————◆———————

A life well-lived is to die for

One would prefer to rest in peace
before death

———————◆———————

Take your time too often and you'll be
left with no time to take

Death is a once-in-a-lifetime experience

Truth drugs are a form of
forced entry

Cremation stops you taking your
secrets to the grave

Being high as a kite comes with
strings attached

The amateur liar avoids your eye;
the professional liar seeks it

Not every hangman gets the
hang of gallows humour

Pity the pensioner who started with
nothing and has most of it left

The human scalp remains a
hair-raising trophy of war

Refuse to play ball and you invite a kicking

DARK

In a democracy, it's ideas that are
flogged to death;
in an autocracy, it's people

Those who hate being a nuisance
can't avoid dying

———————◆———————

Death comes as a rude awakening

———————◆———————

Murder is the ultimate form of theft

———————◆———————

Friends can let you down;
enemies never do

History teaches us that we
rarely learn from it

There is nothing more life-enhancing
than waking up after dreaming
you were dead

DARK

Virtue can be boring; sin never is

A politician's thick skin is mostly scar tissue

The straight-and-narrow
is paved with tablets of stone

---◆---

High unemployment doesn't preclude a
criminal career being open to everyone

---◆---

It's hard to kick the bucket
when popping your clogs

The plagiarist hack never runs out of copy

Unlike humans, vultures do not
prey on the living

Death breathes new life
into immortality

DARK

Prolonged self-neglect is the
politest form of suicide

Funerals are for the living

Only in war is wilful homicide
not called murder

———————◆———————

We can borrow another's sorrows,
but we can never own them

———————◆———————

Torture raises war to a new low

———————◆———————

Bombing from a great height
distances guilt

Persistence is no virtue in a stalker

Reality, like the sun,
can never be faced for long

Feed on others' misfortunes
and you'll never go hungry

A man must stoop very low
to commit high treason

DARK

One is best blown away by ideas,
not bombs

Most unholy wars are dressed up
as holy ones

The bankrupt business school puts its
curriculum into question

For the underprivileged,
life is full of no-entry signs

Depression is best left to the weather

Prostitutes are paid to go public
with their private parts

DARK

The thought of a triple bypass
can make you lose heart

———————◆———————

Life is too short to rush

———————◆———————

Confession is when you come clean
over dirty deeds

Funerals keep the old on the
social circuit

Broken promises cannot be
put in plaster

Most adulterers handle stolen goods

Humour

In old age, we lose height,
but gain authority

Many can't stand taking things
sitting down

To the shyster, fare avoidance
is just the ticket

Footing the bill is hard when it costs
an arm and a leg

Everyone has character;
the question is, which one?

God save us from the
unrebellious teenager

HUMOUR

Food has a habit of going off
while staying put

Given enough notice,
anyone can appear spontaneous

If you believe you can catch up with your
emails, you'll believe anything

All prayers are answered, mostly by silence

We're only old once

Things that go without saying
are invariably said

Dress to kill and you'll have
no admirers

If you can't tell a book by its cover,
sack the designer

Secrets are only safe with the forgetful

Politicians don't need alcohol
to get it wrong - but it helps

We are only as old as our knees

To the procrastinator, there is no
time like the future

Faint praise claps with one hand

Narcissists have only themselves to praise

Would that work-in-progress
always meant progress in work

The Law of Gravity never lets you down

Only lovers know how to rub each
other up the right way

———————◆———————

If your neighbour's music be the food of love,
soundproof your walls

Sugar daddies have a sweet tooth
for crumpet

———————◆———————

Not all old bags remain on the shelf

Coffee is not everyone's cup of tea

Dad's army will fight
denture-and-nail for its country

Deprive a camel of water
and it'll get the hump

Those who fancy themselves don't always
find their interest reciprocated

If the camera never lies, it can be wildly economical with the truth

———————◆———————

Pity the man who doesn't delight in taking offence

———————◆———————

Better fire in the belly than wind

———————◆———————

The man in love with himself need never fear divorce

All marriages are arranged

Food rarely disagrees
with us silently

If money can't buy you happiness,
buy something else

Freeloading passive smokers
save a fortune

The English language is a labyrinth
whose designer lost the key

A repeated joke is like tonic without the gin

Junk food broadens the belly
and narrows the arteries

Removing their make-up
causes some women to lose face

If you must be a victim, at least be a victim
of your own success

Couples should know the ropes
before tying the knot

Dressing young adds years
to the older man

If sex weren't fun,
we wouldn't be here to enjoy it

Lovers mostly make hay
while the moon shines

The older a man gets, the fitter he was

All children are brought up with a
not-to-do list

A man-eating tiger is guilty of
sexual discrimination

Off-centre

Most big talkers act small

Hypochondriacs feel at their best
when ill

Deferring pleasure
can itself be a pleasure

Insults are best swallowed, if not digested

At least corrupt politicians are sincere
in their desire to appear honest

With global warming,
our planet is skating on thin ice

Guilt gives pleasure its seasoning

God without religion is like
Time without a clock

The best questions are those
one shouldn't ask

You have to stay on top of a problem
to get to the bottom of it

To the prisoner,
it's never later than you think

We should cultivate our enemies as assiduously as we cultivate our friends

The trouble with experts is that they know exactly what they are doing

An all-consuming passion doesn't so much burn you out as light you up

Rare is the man whose success is
not built on failure

There is no clear conscience
without a bad memory

Knowledge is too often mistaken
for intelligence

Before taking advice, one should first
take advice about the adviser

Shows of strength are often
a sign of weakness

Horses must see the motor car as liberation,
not competition

We only covet a bull's horns when
we see red

The least funny are those who try to be

A foul-weather friend puts his
fair-weather cousin in the shade

Good manners clothe manipulation
in Sunday best

Youth, like money,
is valued when lost

Mobile phones bolster society's
new life support system

To love one's enemies is the
sweetest form of revenge

A man's downfall captivates us
no less than his rise

Love your work
and leisure becomes an interruption

To say: 'you know what I mean' is
to take the listener for a psychic

Energy is possessed by the young
and valued by the old

Legislators who are a law unto
themselves ignore their own laws

Those with no fixed abode can find their
problems unaddressed

Thinking big comes hard
to the small-minded

In the desert,
you can't move for space

Only think outside the box
if you can deliver inside it

Children can be held back by being
pushed forward

Acting presidential is often just that

A politician's elastic relationship
with the truth is further stretched by the
pull of power

Having the world at your feet
can go to your head

It's often beyond our means
to live within them

Scandal puts flesh
on a man's skeletons

Aim high and you may have to
stoop low to get there

You don't need to know your place
to have one

No one gets charged for
stealing the headlines

Try your hand at something new
and you risk putting your foot in it

If only all history could be
recorded in a black box

Those who see red view things
in black and white

The best way to do it can often be not to

Explanations are rarely innocent

Wisdom

It's a mistake to make mistakes
we can't learn from

A man on his high horse
risks being kicked

Not all who are plugged in
are switched on

Silence is too often mistaken for criticism

Grabbing a person's attention
is easy; keeping hold of it
is more difficult

The grass will grow under your feet
if your head is buried in the sand

WISDOM

Successful skiers spend their lives
going downhill

———————◆———————

Rock the boat too hard and you fall out

———————◆———————

Ask for trouble
and your request will usually be granted

———————◆———————

Those on a bender
can't think straight

Live in an ivory tower and you can't
avoid having your head in the clouds

Yes-men will happily take no
for an answer

Putting your back into it can put it out

No armour-plated vest protects us
from the killer question

Keeping to the straight-and-narrow
can drive one round the bend

Let the cat out of the bag
and you'll be clawed

Drown your enemies in love and
they'll never forgive you

Those who are made for each other
don't always make it

You don't have to be moral
to give moral support

Avoiding stress can be
quite stressful

WISDOM

Worry is usually about something
we can't control

It is small, not great
minds, that think alike

Bending over backwards to do something
does not always take you forward

It takes an empty vessel to be full of itself

Age prevention does not equate to
youth restoration

Keep someone on a tight leash
and they'll feel at a loose end

Posthumous fame is a dead end

Life's drama keeps us guessing
up to the final curtain

Respect can be earned, but never bought

◆

Less is more - but it takes longer

◆

Without obstacles,
there is little achievement

◆

Time doesn't go faster
just because the clock is ticking

Chase happiness and,
like the far horizon, it eludes you

Humility is to eat the egg that's thrown at you

Tall stories are best kept short

Fences are best mended
behind closed doors

WISDOM

The sure-footed provide a safe pair
of hands

Play ball with people and you'll have
a good run for your money

Pushing the envelope
puts your stamp on it

If you can't stand someone, just sit on them

Life is too short to drink the house wine

Only re-invent yourself if you can
afford to buy the patent

Only laugh at yourself if you are funny

One should always be awake
to the onset of insomnia

WISDOM

Middle age is when you conceal your age;
old age is when you conceal your children's

———————◆———————

There is no vaccination against the travel bug

———————◆———————

Corrupt states risk drowning
in the vinegar of their rotten apples

Ignorance is easier to live with
than uncertainty

It's one thing to pick up the pieces,
quite another to reassemble them

Nothing comes out of nowhere

WISDOM

Bibliography

Me

Notes

Notes

Notes

Notes